The Wonderful World of Birds

How to Make Friends

With Our Feathered Friends

Nature Learning Series
Dueep J Singh
Mendon Cottage Books

JD-Biz Publishing

Download Free Books!

http://MendonCottageBooks.com

Our books are available at

1. Amazon.com
2. Barnes and Noble
3. Itunes
4. Kobo
5. Smashwords
6. Google Play Books

Table of Contents

Introduction

Did you know that some of the birds which people believed would never ever be extinct because they were so numerous have disappeared in the 20th and the 21st century? The last passenger pigeon, which once covered the skies of North America, died in captivity in 1904. In the same manner, it took just five years to kill off all the vultures, the Kites, the Eagles and the house sparrow (*Passer Domesticus*) and many other birds once common in cities, in parts of the Indian subcontinent. Blame it all on pesticides and also humans encroaching the natural habitats of birds.

So why should you be interested in the wonderful world of birds, you may ask? Well, it is a well-known fact that a number of bird species are disappearing from the face of the earth, just like the Great Auk and the dodo at the rate of 10- *25 per year.* So what, you may say, after all, there are so many other birds to choose from. Just calculate. 25 species going extinct per year, never to make their appearance on earth again. At this rate, we are not going to see a living bird in the next 50 to 75 years. That is reality. There may come a generation, which may ask its grandparents, "what were those silly little creatures, you called birds? We can just hear their songs on audio. What were they like to look at?" And the grandparents trying desperately to describe the magic world of birds.

Imagine a world without nightingales singing in Berkeley Square, bluebirds flying over the white cliffs of Dover, peacocks in purple adorning and other such songbirds disappearing from your windowsill, garden and lives. Imagine no bird nesting in your garden or waking you up to birdsong, bright and early in the morning. So if you begin to take an interest in birds, there is a chance that you may want to help save them and your children might grow up to be keen ornithologists.

Knowing More about the Birds around You – Fun Facts of the More Common Bird Species

All About Blackbirds

Male blackbird

The Common Blackbird , usually known simply as a "Blackbird ", is a part of the Thrush bird family. Unlike many other birds that are native to just one or two continents, the Blackbird breeds in North Africa, Asia, and Europe. It has even begun to breed recently in Australia. Please do not confuse a blackbird with a crow or with a Raven. They are literally black birds – due to their color – but a common blackbird is a different breed altogether.

The Blackbird typically measures between 23.5 centimeters to 29 centimeters. They usually weigh between 2.8 and 4.4 ounces. Males and females usually differ in appearance. The male has black-brown legs and orange-yellow bill that gets darker during the winter months, and a glossy black plumage. On the other hand, a female Blackbird has a dull yellow-brownish bill, a sooty brown color, and a bit of mottling on its breast.

A male Blackbird is very aggressive when it comes to defending its territory. If they feel as though their territory is being threatened, they do something called a "bow and run." Basically, what this entails is a short run in which the head is first raised and then bowed in quick little jerks. During this time, the bird will dip its tail. When a fight goes down, it is usually a short challenging fight and the intruder is quick to run away.

As far as diet goes, the Blackbird is an omnivore. Their diet includes earthworms, berries, seeds, and many kinds of insects. They usually feed on the ground, running and hopping to grab their food. If they choose to eat fruits, they can grab what is on the ground and will sometimes even go into people's gardens to grab goodies.

The call and song of a Blackbird varies, depending on its purpose. For instance, if the bird is looking to scare away potential enemies, they will make a "*pook-pook-pook* " sound. If it wants to defend its territory from other Blackbird s, it will make a "*chink-chink*" noise.

Unlike many other birds, the Blackbird species is nowhere near extinct. In fact, the population seems to be growing, thriving and multiplying vigorously. This means they should be around for a long time!

Amazing Sparrow Facts

The most familiar of all birds, sparrows thrive all over the world. The three main groups are the true sparrows, the snowfinches, and the rock sparrows. These are separate and distinct from the American sparrow. You may take them for granted but after reading these facts, you will be amazed at how versatile this bird really is.

1. Sparrows can live just about anywhere.

There have been sparrow sightings in many diverse locations. Entire groups have lived out their lives under the shelter of enormous industrial warehouses. Cavers discovered a large population 2,000 feet underground in an old coal mine. As long as they can build nests and find food, these birds can make a go of it and survived, even though you cannot find them in the densely populated areas of the Indian subcontinent.

2. Sparrows are notorious for sneaking outside the bonds of monogamy.

Researchers report that up to 28% of all eggs are the product of a female sparrow and a male sparrow who is not her breeding partner. Scientists are puzzled by this behavior. Females with extra-pair offspring have fewer total offspring than their monogamous friends. However, more of the young from extra-pair matings make it to breeding age.

3. House sparrows mostly feed on seeds and other plant matter but in the springtime they can be found busily gathering insects.

Those insects are for the young sparrows. Newly hatched sparrows require more protein and their parents work hard to provide it for them. Living in large flocks, the parents must compete with others for access to the best food for their young. Why this hurry? Sparrow chicks must be ready to fly from the nest within two weeks of hatching.

male sparrow

In some ways, the large sparrow population is due to the progress of human beings especially in the matters of building cities and constructing houses over what was once forestland. They prefer building their nests in man-made structures and love living near their human counterparts. Readily adaptable, they are able to find plenty to eat in the foodstuff we discard or make available to them in our gardens and parks.

Astounding Facts and Information About Hawks

A very unique bird that many people have seen throughout their lives is the Hawk. Hawks are a very unique species of bird, one of the most formidable birds of prey in the world today.

Although they may look slightly different, Hawks are actually part of the same family as vultures, ospreys, and falcons. They have the ability to capture their prey, and tear it apart, using their very sharp curved beaks and talons. These birds also have exceptional eyesight, something that allows them to hunt from high above, sighting and pouncing upon their unsuspecting prey below. You have probably seen them soaring above you at great altitudes, something that they can do for long periods of time.

Red Tailed Hawk in flight

Female hawks are typically much stronger and larger than their male counterparts. Although they are typically reddish-brown on top, and white beneath, they can also be gray in color. You will usually see darker spots or even streaks on their neck. You will see darker bars of color on their wings and tails. Their legs can be feathered all the way down to their toes, and their black talons are very noticeable against the background of yellow feet. In most cases, Hawks can be seen hunting during the day, usually seeking smaller birds or even land animals. There are some species that hunt at night – such as the Bat Hawk – and most of them do not hunt livestock on farms or other areas where domesticated animals are found.

You have probably seen hawks perching on poles or wires, quickly bolting into the air quickly when they see something on the ground. They are capable of making extremely sharp turns even at high speeds, something that makes them very formidable hunters regardless of the location and habitat. Hawks will pounce upon their prey, unless they are able to capture it in midair. In order to stay healthy and active, they must eat at least 25% of their body weight each day.

They can often be seen at the edge of the lake or stream bathing to keep their feathers in a top and sleek condition. Like most birds, they have oil that naturally coats their feathers, making them waterproof and helping them to fly. When they build a nest, they will do so either in trees, or on rocky cliffs to keep their young safe from harm.

Facts About The Cranes

There are 15 species of cranes. This large bird is found on every continent except in South America and in Antarctica. Their beauty and size have made these birds the stuff of legend and fairy tales. Many members of this species are endangered as the amount of available natural habitats continues to decrease.

1. The Japanese consider the crane to be a National Treasure.

Japanese fables use the crane as an example and symbol of longevity. Legends state that a crane can live for 1,000 years and symbolizes fidelity since cranes mate for life. The Red Crowned crane was thought to be extinct, but a few have been found. Efforts to increase the amount of available wetlands for breeding have been put in place and the numbers are slowly rising.

Sandhill Cranes

2. The migratory Sandhill crane is the most common crane in the world.

An omnivorous feeder, the Sandhill crane will eat whatever is available, including tubers, worms, and even snakes. Cranes are fantastic dancers. During the mating ritual, they cavort and sing in unison. Naturally grey with a crimson crown, they are known to apply mud and dirt to their feathers and may appear to be brown.

3. Whooping cranes can reach height of five feet when mature.

Although the Whooping Crane is a flocking bird, there are only two to three birds in a group during migration. They stuff themselves with blue crabs to fatten up prior to leaving for their winter breeding grounds. Birds commonly head for Texas and Florida but a new refuge has been created for them in Louisiana. Their long necks and a wingspan of up to 7.5 feet make them spectacular in flight.

Many cranes are on the endangered species list. The earliest fossil records give an estimated age of ten million years for this remarkable bird. If you ever get the chance to see one in flight, consider yourself lucky.

Facts about the Goldfinch

The Goldfinch is one of the more colorful and gregarious of North American birds. It is a small bird (approximately 5 inches in length) who tends to stand out because of his bright lemon yellow body, white undertail and black wings and cap. Of course, as with a majority of bird species, the male is the more colorful. The female, however, is not without her own beauty, leaning more toward an olive green coloring with touches of yellow and white in her undertail.

Male Goldfinch

The goldfinch generally resides along country roads and in brushy fields and feeds on seeds and grains. He generally can be found in large flocks that swoop and climb the air streams, a treat to the eye for those fortunate enough to run across a flock in flight.

They are social birds, but also territorial when it comes to nesting. They are often found in residential areas and are attracted to bird feeders offering thistle and black sunflower seeds. Once they have discovered your feeders, you are in for a treat! Goldfinches are the ultimate "eye candy" of the bird world!

If you want to attract goldfinches, a good and easily accessible water source is vital, as these birds love a nice bath. Also, in summertime, you might tempt them with a garden offering such treats as Thistle, Coreopsis, Zinnias and berries. Quite often the female returns to build her nest in the same location from year to year. So, if you play your cards right, you will have a friend for life!

A bit of advice about feeders: if you have a lot of squirrels in your yard, go with a mesh feeder. It's harder for squirrels to master, whereas they will destroy the plastic tube type feeder. Also, clean the feeder out after a heavy rain or the goldfinches will not return to it.

Facts and Information About Ducks

You have probably seen ducks flying by, or floating in the water at a nearby pond in your area. There are many different breeds of ducks, coming in a wide variety of colors. Finding information about these wonderful animals can be a rewarding experience, something that you can do on your own, or as a project done with friends and family. If you are interested in ducks, and would like to know a little bit more about them, here are some quick facts about ducks that you ought to know.

Depending upon where you live, you have probably seen ducks in both freshwater and in salt water settings. This is because they can be found in both. These wild, and sometimes domesticated, web footed birds are very common in many places, usually possessing very short legs and depressed bodies that are designed for both flying and swimming. Part of the Anatidae family, these beautiful birds have many different species, but can be easily divided between sea ducks and river ducks. More specifically, they can be further subdivided into South American, Muscovy, China, and wood ducks.

Muscovy ducks

Ducks can live from three years all the way up to a couple decades depending upon their species. They weigh between 7 and 9 pounds and can grow up to 20 inches in length. They have a traditional diet of worms, insects, fish, grass, and even certain tree leaves.

Most duck species are monogamous, only breeding once a year. If you look closely, the wings of a duck are very pointed and short, giving them great strength for both long and short distance flights. Male ducks are called

Drake. Females are simply referred to as a Duck. Baby ducks are, of course, called ducklings, and when a large group of them together is called a Brace. This cursory overview of ducks should help you get a better understanding of this beautiful bird.

Domesticated ducks are rather silly birds. Many of them have this bad habit of laying their eggs in the water, – especially if they have been swimming throughout the day – or in really inaccessible places like under shrubs or in brushwood. So if you are raising ducks as providers of eggs, you need to make sure that they have places on land where they can they can lay their eggs. After that, they can be released to swim in the pond.

Facts and Information on Blue Jays

Blue Jays are a fairly common sight in North America, but that doesn't make them any less interesting to those fond of watching birds. Their cleverness is legendary. They are adaptable and intelligent birds, capable of imitating the sounds of many of their feathered contemporaries.

They are capable of outwitting them as well. Blue Jays are notorious for stealing eggs from the nests of other birds, as well as their nestlings. As humans, that doesn't register well on our sympathy scale, but it's the way of nature and serves to keep things in balance. And don't forget, even blue jays have their share of predators to fear.

Blue Jays are attracted to acorns, nuts and seeds, as well as small critters such as grasshoppers, caterpillars and beetles. If you live in a wooded area and feel you're being swallowed up by the forest, you have Blue Jays, in part, to thank for it. They are hoarders of acorns, but have a tendency to transfer them somewhere - like your front yard - and then fail to retrieve them. The result is a yard full of oak trees you hadn't planned on, blocking your view and preventing the sun from getting through.

There are over 40 species of Jays worldwide, eight of which are common to North America. Many consider the "Jaybird" more of a pest than anything else, but it can also be a big help in ridding your yard of pests. It's fun to watch a blue jay at your bird feeder rigorously shaking the peanuts you have put out to determine which shells still contain nuts.

Winter Blue Jay

Blue Jays do migrate in the winter, but this is not a consistent pattern. Some winters find them toughing it out in the snow and cold right along with the rest of us. Scientists as yet have found no explanation for this phenomenon.

Facts and Information on Chickadees

Black-capped Chickadees (poecile atricapilla) on a branch

Chickadees may be one of the more commonly known of the North American birds, but there is nothing "common" about these charming creatures. In fact, you'll have a challenge ahead of you if you want to check off all the different species of chickadee from your life list. Several to watch for are the black-capped chickadee, the Carolina chickadee, the Mountain Chickadee, the Boreal and the chestnut back chickadee.

Most chickadees nest in the cavities of trees and bushes, and are especially fond of rotten or decaying wood. But, the lazier among them aren't above poaching an old woodpecker hole or a "pre-owned" nesting box! The mountain chickadee may even choose a hole in the ground or crevice in a rock formation as his home.

If you want to attract chickadees to your feeder, load up with sunflower seeds or sunflower hearts. You might also offer them some chopped walnuts. You can even hand-feed these little guys. Just stand close to the bird feeder and stretch out your arm with palm flattened and an offering of seeds or nuts. Then wait very quietly. Your patience will be rewarded with a very quick but satisfying visit from your dinner guest. In and out like a puff of air touching your out-stretched hand.

But chickadees are very self-sufficient little creatures who get only about 20% of their winter food from feeders. The rest they find by foraging in the foliage of bushes and trees for spiders and larvae.

Some chickadees, such as the Mountain Chickadee, are only found in the West and particularly - you guessed it - in the mountains (the Rockies to be exact). The Mexican Chickadee is indigenous to New Mexico and Arizona. But wherever you live, you can count on enjoying visits from at least some species of Chickadee.

Facts and Information on Egrets

If you have ever seen one of these majestic creatures floating gracefully through the air, you will understand the attraction of the Egret. You will find these large white birds with their long wing-span mostly in wetlands and marshy areas, such as the swamps and marshes of North and South Carolina. Nevertheless they are water birds, and are attracted to most any habitat that offers a decent water source.

Egrets share their habitat with other birds attracted to a watery environment, such as blue herons. In fact, they are a part of the heron family.

There are several types of egrets, Great White Snowy and Cattle Egrets. They build their nests in trees and gather with other wetland birds in colonies. An egret launching itself airborne, stretching its great wings to their full length, is a sight to behold!

The egret's elegance and tenacity to survive made it the perfect symbol for the National Audubon Society. It wasn't that long ago that these beautiful creatures were facing extinction due to the great demand for their large white feathers by the fashion industry. In the late 19th century one could see more of the egrets' beautiful plumage in ladies' hats than on the bird itself. Peacock and ostrich tail feathers plumes have also been much in vogue.

Only 5% of the egret population remained when legislation was finally enacted to protect this lovely creature from extinction! Thankfully, egrets are now once again plentiful and will remain so with proper monitoring and continued protection.

Their diet consists mostly of fish, which they skillfully hunt in their wetland habitat by standing or wading through shallow water to catch unsuspecting fish with a quick jab of their long yellow bills.

Egrets are easy to identify with these bills, their long necks and soft white plumage. An outing to the tidal wetlands of the Carolinas will pretty much guarantee a sighting of these lovely creatures.

Great Blue Heron Ardea herodias - Fort Myers Beach

Facts and information about Vultures

When you want to learn more about the many birds in the animal kingdom, the vulture is not a bad place to start. You can learn many facts and get more information about vultures, so that you understand their habits and what they are all about. If you have watched television or read any story involving vultures, they're probably depicted there as an omen of death. This is because they are carnivorous and often scavenge for meat, rather than doing any hunting themselves. For this reason, they circle above when an animal has died or is about to die. These birds typically live on off of this carrion, rather than gathering their own food. They are also found on all the continents on the earth except for Antarctica and Australia.

Endangered California condor flying

They tend to stick to themselves, as opposed to congregating in large groups. They are also known for their strong senses, particularly a strong sense of smell and sight. They are thorough when it comes to stripping other animals for food, as they often do not leave any pieces behind except the bones. When you want to learn more about these birds, you should find a source of information in your local library or on the Internet that gives great details about them.

If that is what you were looking for, a good biology Journal is a good place to start. A lot has been written about these birds, and their unique abilities. If you are a bird lover or just someone who loves learning more about animals, this could be a keen endeavor for you upon which to embark. Vultures have had a bad reputation down the ages, so that many people do not know much about them, but if you're looking to learn more, you should make sure that you take advantage of the plentiful information that has been written about them. This will provide you with what you need when you want to know more about this tough and adaptable bird.

Fun Facts About Falcons

A falcon perched on its trainers hand

Falcons are found all over the world with more than 60 known species of this bird of prey. Commonly confused with hawks, falcons have long and pointed wings built for speed and aerial maneuvers. Their bills are notched instead of smooth like the bill of Hawks. Here are some amazing and fun facts about falcons to share with your friends and family.

1. Gyrfalcons are able to live and hunt in Arctic regions.

The gyrfalcon is the undisputed royal bird in the falcon family. The largest of all falcons, it could only be used by a king in the hunt. This fabulous bird lives in cold areas and can be found nesting in Arctic areas. In some cases, gyrfalcons lay their eggs in freezing temperatures.

2. Faster than a speeding bullet, the peregrine falcon has been clocked at speeds of more than 200 mph during a dive.

Unsurprisingly, this bird is a great hunter and was once the most common daytime predatory bird in the world. As habitat has changed, peregrine falcons have moved to the cities. Commonly spotted flying around skyscrapers, they hunt pigeons and other small prey. Populations of this raptor are growing and it is no longer on the Endangered Species List.

3. The Merlin is also known as a pigeon hawk.

Falcons and Merlins were tamed by the aristocracy during medieval times. Many tapestries have ladies carrying Merlins on their leather – gloved hands, while riding out on a hunt. Ladies of the European courts frequently flew the trained Merlin during the hunt. Resembling a pigeon during flight, it is smaller than the peregrine falcon and almost as fast. This fierce bird is in constant motion and rarely glides. It patrols open spaces such as meadows and shorelines to find small birds and even dragonflies on which it feeds.

A Peregrine Falcon (Falco peregrinus) perched on a stump.

Falcons are incredible hunters and have been used for sport for many generations. Their keen intelligence and hunting skills are appreciated by all who watch them soar through the air.

Fun Facts and Information about Gulls

Herring Gull

One of the most beautiful birds – and among the noisiest –that you will ever see is a seagull. Also known as gulls, these very clever birds can be seen both inland, and most commonly near coastal regions. They have many unique characteristics that set them apart from typical birds that you have probably seen flying by. Here are a few fun facts about gulls that you might find interesting.

A very unique characteristic about gulls is their wide range of feeding habits. Although you will often see them diving into the waters to capture an occasional fish, they are much more clever than you would expect. For instance, if they are able to get a hard shelled mollusk, they will actually take it several yards into the sky, dropping it onto rocks in order to break it open. They also may be seen in fields that have recently been plowed, finding upturned grubs that are one of their favorite sources of food. They may even stomp the ground, imitating rainfall, tricking earthworms to rise to the surface.

Gulls are one of the few birds that can actually drink both freshwater and saltwater. They are born with special glands above their eyes which allows them to flush the salt from seawater that they drink. They are also known to have the ability to communicate with each other, using both body movements and vocalizations that are some form of communication. When they mate, they mate for life, and actually take turns to incubate their eggs. Although they look very similar, there is a considerable amount of diversity between the different species of gulls. Some of them are very small, reaching only 1 foot in length. The larger ones are between 2 and 3 feet in size, weighing almost 4 pounds each.

They are also able to conserve their energy by gliding, and absorb energy from paved roadways during the cold seasons. They are also very fond of crickets, and have been represented by both the settlers of Utah, and Native Americans, as symbols that represent both versatility and freedom. These dynamic birds are definitely unique, possessing both beauty and dynamic qualities in order to survive and flourish.

Information and Facts About Finches

Finches are little birds belonging to the same Passeridae Group as the Sparrow and it is easy to miss spotting them, yet they are among the most popular, the most widely observed, and the most popular of pet birds in the world, especially Gold Finches. Many people would rather have a finch as a pet than a parrot or a parakeet. There is much to learn about these tiny, little happy birds.

While it is a fact that most pet birds, such as parrots and parakeets need some kind of human socialization in order to thrive in captivity, finches would rather have the company of other finches, and as far as those humans go, they could take them or leave them. They should be kept in pairs or in groups, and if they are kept individually, they can get physically and mentally unstable, to the point of becoming depressed.

It is customary to handle parrots and parakeets, but not finches. Finches would **rather not be handled** and they should be touched as little as possible to avoid causing them stress and frightening them. So handle the Finches as little as possible to keep them happy.

Finches are among the smallest of the small birds, only weighing less than an ounce and measuring less than 4 inches from beak to tail feathers. While some people might think that this small bird would be the perfect bird for small, cozy homes, quite the opposite is true, as you might need a bigger cage for Finches than for Parrots. Finches have to be able to fly, and the more the merrier. They really need a larger area in a cage to enable them to fly around.

Finches love to sing and chirp, but their tiny voices are so faint they make good choices for people who live in small houses or apartments. Their happy chirp cannot even be heard outside of the room in which they live, and people who have them enjoy their pleasant, happy voices.

Zebra Finches

Interesting Facts and Information about Owls

Owls are nocturnal predatory birds. This particular bird genus and species belongs to the bird Order – Strigiformes. A nocturnal predator like an owl likes to hunt for its prey at night.

There are two kinds of owls, barn owls and true owls. True owls have about 190 species while there are only about 16 species of barn owls.

Here are some more interesting facts about owls.

Owls cannot move their eyes very much. For this reason, they have developed the ability to turn their heads completely in order to see well. Owls' eyes face forward, so they must use their enhanced sense of binocular sight to find their prey, which includes mammals and insects. Some owls enjoy hunting fish.

Owls are flight birds yet they fly in a silent manner. This is due to the heavy structure of their feathers. Also, the fact that owls hunt mostly at night contributes to their quiet flight. They intend to catch up with their unaware prey which does not know anything about their silent approach and swoop.

Owls –like all other birds-have no teeth with which to eat or chew their prey. They swallow their prey whole. They use their talons, or claws, to clutch and kill their prey. After about six hours, they will regurgitate some of their food, and use it to help make nests, among other things.

It is important to know that owls do not actually make their own nests. They make use of nests made by other birds. Owls come in colors like brown and tan, but they tend to become whatever color their surroundings are most of all. They need to blend into their surroundings in order to camouflage themselves from the prey that they seek.

Owls are found in every continent except Antarctica. When an owl is part of a group of owls, that group is called a parliament. A Parliament of owls! Amusing choice of words, if taken literally.

Barn Owl

Song of the baby barn Owl

As I sit meditating on the branch of a tree,

Those humans look fascinated up at me.

They contemplate my sober and solemn aspect

With awe, reverence and respect.

They gaze into my wide eyes

And murmur, "how grave.""How wise…"

Grave and wise? I ? What a suggestion!

While I'm thinking, "To fly or not to Fly? That is the question…"

How absurd!

I am just a flibberty-gibberty willow th'wispy giddy young Bird.

Territorial Rights of Birds

Did you know that the idea of "as free as a bird" is totally wrong? Birds are not free. They are prisoners of the land they fly over. They are slaves to the air they fly through. They are bound with instinctive limits, which prevent them from going over an area which is some other bird's territory.

Birds establish territories with their neighboring birds. A bird cannot enter another bird's territory unless it wants a quarrel on its hands. These boundaries are established in the minds of the birds, and they cannot fly through them. So if a bird's territory is destroyed through man-made calamities like forest brush and bushes being cleared and trees being chopped down, the birds cannot ask for shelter in another bird's territory. So they stay and die in their own area.

Why are birds more devoted to a piece of ground in comparison to other animals? That is because this helps them find their own made sense set up their new homes. The need for their own space leads young couples to spread out and establish their own area. Thus their own kind of bird species becomes widely scattered and has a better chance to survive. The bigger and stronger the male bird is, the larger his territory area will be.

Why do some birds make their nests in just one particular place? That is because they have mapped out that territory as their own. So a bird which stays in one place is not going to from its territory. On the other hand, migratory birds have their own territories to which they come back in summer and in winter.

Migratory birds normally work together so that they can protect their general territory against other groups of their own species trying to encroach on their land. But, surprisingly enough, they will allow birds of a different species to nest or live on their territory, because they are not in competition with each other. However, a dove , which is supposed to be the symbol of peace and which happens to be one of the most quarrelsome of birds will not allow another dove to make its nest on its territory. But it will allow a robin, a hummingbird, or a wren to build a nest and raise its family in its territory.

How do birds stake out land?

Natural impulses and instincts are inborn and that is why birds have managed to survive for millenniums because of these highly developed instincts. A male bird stakes out land by alighting on a branch and singing.

If he has no challenger answering his Birdsong, that territory is his. He then marks the boundaries of the land that he can defend. However, if he is challenged by another male bird stopping him from marking out his boundaries, he is going to move back a shrub or two.

A bird normally just has that much land in which he can raise a family safely. That is why he is going to look for that land on which the food is plentiful and the protection is more than adequate. A female is going to select her mate after she has inspected the land he has staked out as his own. Weaker males are going to remain bachelors.

Different species claim different amounts of territory. Eagles and owls may have land covering several square miles. On the other hand, Penguins and seagulls take only about a square foot or so of land on which they can build their nests.

Have you seen air to air fights between two birds? These birds may seem to rise and slide down some invisible wall in the air. After that, the birds fly into branches on their own territory and talk to each other, establishing the boundary area. Once that has been set out, both burst into happy Birdsong. You happy, I happy, I will not bother you. As long as you do not bother me.

You may ask why smaller birds are not very worried, when larger and more predatory birds stake out areas which cover their own land. Just imagine that you are a little sparrow or a little wren. And suddenly your area has been staked out by a hawk. What do you do then?

Birds do not fly on any course haphazardly, while covering land. They have their own aerial routes. So as long as the hawk's feeding spot is not in your territory, little sparrow or little wren, you do not need to worry. This natural traveling through the air on a regular route means that small bird populations can mark out the routes and then rest assured when and where and if they face danger from larger birds and also how they can live happily ever after in their own safe, secure and sound territory.

In the same way you may notice that birds roost far away from their nests, unless they are incubating their eggs. That is when they get together in a secure area, where they know that they are protected and among other birds of their species. That is why if you are living in the wilderness, you may have noticed all these birds getting together at dusk and communicating with each other. Who knows, they may be comparing notes on the day's work, Human watching to tell each other about all the exciting habits of those creatures called humans. Then early in the morning, it is the same thing again – Birdsong and telling each other what they intend to do during the day.

Birds normally roost in their own chosen places, along with their friends.

One question a youngster asked me was how come birds do not fall off their branches when they are fast asleep. That is because they hold their position on the branches with their claws'"interlocking grip". It is almost like a hand fisting over a stick and holding on for dear life. That is also the reason why birds do not get blown away during sudden gusts of wind and rain during night. They just fluff out their feathers and hope for the best. The feathers, of course, are the best insulating blankets which keep them warm. Nevertheless, it is a good thing if you provide your feathered friends with shelter and that is why the next chapter is going to concentrate on how to make bird houses for our pals.

And in believing, it is easy. Even a seven-year-old child can do that!

How to Make Bird Houses

I ended the previous chapter by telling you that a seven-year-old child could make a bird house for a bird. Well, I did that when I was seven so QED.

How did I make this birdhouse? We lived in an area which had plenty of coconut trees, so I had this extra and dry coconut in hand. I just made a hole with a screwdriver on the top of the coconut. Then I made a larger hole with the screwdriver on the side of the coconut – under the supervision of my father, who made sure that the screwdriver did not slip and had already cracked the coconut a bit so that a small portion could be removed from the side.) I was making a rough and ready birdhouse for my bird friends. I was not bothered about circles, which can be drilled on sides of coconuts. [I did not have a drill, then nor do I have one now! Consider me primitive.] I did not bother removing the coconut meat from inside the coconut because I wanted my friends to have something to eat. [I drank the coconut juice!]

End result – one coconut with two holes hung from a rope as long as you want.

You just need to insert the rope through the top of the coconut and knot it *from inside*. And then you just need to hang it securely on the nearest branch. The coconut meat inside the coconut is going to tempt the birds to enter, eat, and if they have the sense, decide to stay on there. Easy, is not it?

Some people also use these coconut shells as bird feeding tables. Well, that is a good idea. Make a larger hole and add birdseed in the coconut shell. The more coconut shells you have hanging on secure branches in your garden, the more the birds are going to be encouraged in visiting it and staying on…

Feeders

There are a number of bird species who prefer to stay in your garden, eat, drink and then fly away to their nests in the shrubbery. You can hang a feeder for these species from a sturdy branch or just nail a plank on top of a wooden post. Hummingbirds like sweetened water or even anything with honey. Other birds may like a mixture of seeds, grains, cereals, fruit, or any other natural plant product you want to feed them. Squirrels are also going to be attracted to feeders.

Bird houses do not have to be elaborate and stylish. They are not bothered about furnishing; they are more bothered about security. I used the rope, because I was hanging the coconut in an area, which was not buffeted too much by winds. But you can always use wire. The coconut is not going to swing so much, but it is going to stay secure!

If you are a DIY sort of guy, and love constructing bird houses by hand, there are plenty of plans available online. But if you want the basic idea of how to construct a birdhouse, here it is –

First, choose your spot. It should be inaccessible to the birds' natural enemies. These enemies include cats, rodents, and reptiles, and even other bigger birds. That means the entry of the birdhouse should make it impossible for a larger bird to get inside when it is hunting a smaller bird. Along with that, the depth of the house should be so much that a bird can hide away in the farthest corner without its hunter's beak managing to harm it.

You need to mount to this birdhouse on a sturdy pole. That pole can either be of wood or of metal. Do not paint the birdhouse, because that may keep birds away. Leave the wood as it is, in its natural state as far as possible.

Different Styles of Bird Houses

Putting up bird houses is definitely a good idea, especially in areas where natural cover and their usual habitat has been destroyed due to the encroachment of human beings and human inhabitation.

Remember that different styles of bird houses are going to depend on the particular bird species you want to target for nesting in your wooden birdhouse constructions.

First of all you need to see if the area in which you want to place the bird house is favorable for a particular bird species. If you are looking to attract larger birds, but the entrance of the bird house is just large enough for sparrows, robins, wrens and bluebirds, you are not going to find Blue Jays or red cardinals nesting in your bird house.

So use a little bit of common sense and logic and then spend some time researching on the particular habitat which attracts your chosen species of birds. And then start creating that particular atmosphere and environment right in your backyard.

Here are some different types of bird houses-

Letter Box Type Mounted Bird House

One of the most common and popular type of bird houses found out there, a letter box type of bird house is normally placed high up on tree trunks, wooden or metal poles. This bird house has a hinged roof so that can open up the roof and clean it when necessary.

Hanging Bird House

Do you have an old tree in your backyard or in your garden? All you have to do is hang a birdhouse on some of its sturdy branches with the help of a chain. You do not need to spend lots and lots of money making a very expensive and stylish bird house. The coconut example given above is the perfect hanging house.

 In fact, any sort of sturdy wooden or wicker box with a small opening on the top – the entrance – can be used as a hanging bird house. Do not use metal for any sort of bird houses.

Bird house with Open Extensions-

You may want to attach your birdhouse's floor to a sturdy plank. This is going to be the balcony portion of your birdhouse. You can always place plenty of food on that empty plank space. And if some bird decides that it really likes this lifestyle – food right at its doorstep, and a snug and cozy place in which to build its nest, there you are.

Some birds prefer open front entrances so that they can enter and exit their shelter easily. The extension can be as large or as small as you wish. If you want to buy a bird house, look for quality products with proper drainage facilities and ventilation, and roofs or back walls which can be removed easily.

Repeat- Please do not paint your nest boxes, because paint consists of harmful material like creosote and other lead-based items. These are going to harm the birds.

Protect your bird box from predators by coating the metal support pole with a mixture of red pepper and Vaseline. This will dissuade animals from trying to climb up the pole to get to the nesting bird family.

Why Following a Plan Is the Best Way to Build a Bird House

Just imagine that you have spent many happy hours in the backyard watching birds of different species frolicking in the sun. You have even watched them build their nests in the shrubbery and the trees in your garden. And then one fine day you found out that there were plenty of published books and information on the Internet telling you all about plans to build a bird house. That excited you a lot, did not it? But why should you follow somebody else's plan to build that perfect bird house?

Well, here are some good reasons why following a plan is the best way to build a bird house.

Different bird species have different bird house plans built according to their physical characteristics and behavioral specifications. Nevertheless, all of these bird houses are built on some common general patterns, notwithstanding the architectural design, stylish embellishments and other innovative ideas which you would want to implement while building a bird nesting house.

Wood is definitely the best material with which to build a good solid bird house. Wooden planks, especially those with the bark still on them can be easily constructed into a suitable bird house.

Make the birdhouse in such a manner that it is easy to assemble and disassemble. Screws are best to hold the different parts of the birdhouse together. Nailing these different parts together means that you cannot disassemble the birdhouse easily. The little bird is not going to clean up its lodgings. That is your job. That is why you need to construct the birdhouse in such a manner that it can be taken to pieces with the help of a screwdriver and reassembled again when it has been swept and garnished properly.

Make sure that the birdhouses are placed in areas where they are not totally inaccessible to their natural enemies. Predators like cats, rats and owls are always on the lookout for easily accessible nests and bird houses. So these bird boxes are only going to be a success when their occupants feel completely safe when in them.

Special Birdhouse Plans For Different Bird Species

A good bird box plan is going to depend on the requirement of the bird species. You need to take that into view, while choosing the exactly right plans for the birds in your garden. These bird boxes can be mounted on iron poles. This can protect the birds from predators. Some birdhouse designs also use the idea of suspending the houses from wires, high above the ground.

Bird houses should be built and placed at a range of about 150 feet away from human habitation. That assures your bird friends that you are not encroaching in its particular territory.

A plan gives you proper instructions and dimensions necessary to build this house. So even if you are not handy with tools around the house, easy to follow instructions laid out in a step by step and methodical manner can get you trying out your hand at building a bird house this weekend.

Make sure that you have followed all the instructions given in your particular choice of bird house plan in order to make the best wooden, sturdy, durable, waterproof and resilient bird house.

Here are the items needed to construct a bird house-

- A good plan and a vision of how large you want the bird house to be.

    This website has some amazing plans-

    http://www.ohio-nature.com/bird-house-plans.html

However, in the paucity of readily available plans, you can use a little bit of ingenuity and visualize a post box.

- ¾ inch thick planks are the best thickness for constructing bird houses. This is going to keep the little bird family snug especially in inclement weather. Try using pine planks. These are long-lasting, as is Oak, Cedar and other popular woods used for building furniture.

- Two pieces 8 ½" planks
- Two pieces 9" x 6"boards
- One piece – 6 ½" into 7 ½"for the roof.
- One 6" by 6" board for the floor
- Saw, drill, 2 hinges, screwdriver and screws.

Construction instructions

1. Drill holes into the floor board, so that any excessive water can drain out. The roof is going to be sloping, so there is less chance of any leakage through the wooden roof.

2. The 9" x 6" have to be cut at an angle. The front portion should measure 8" but the back portion should still remain 9". These are going to be the sides of the bird house. The angle means that the roof can be placed at a slope.

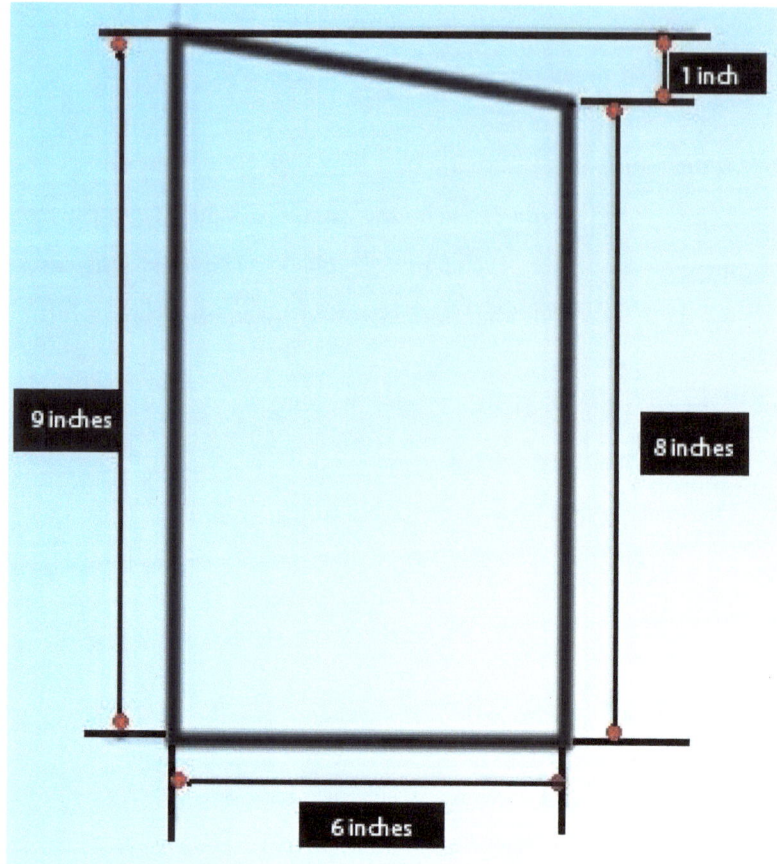

3. Now take the 8 ½ "board. Drill a ½ "diameter hole about seven inches above its floor. This is going to be the entrance. You can also facilitate the babies' entrance and exit through this entrance by making some grooves in the inside portion of the 8 ½ inch board.

4. It is much more sensible to use screws to assemble these pieces. The roof needs to be hinged so that you can open it and clean it up after the birds have left the nest.

End Result

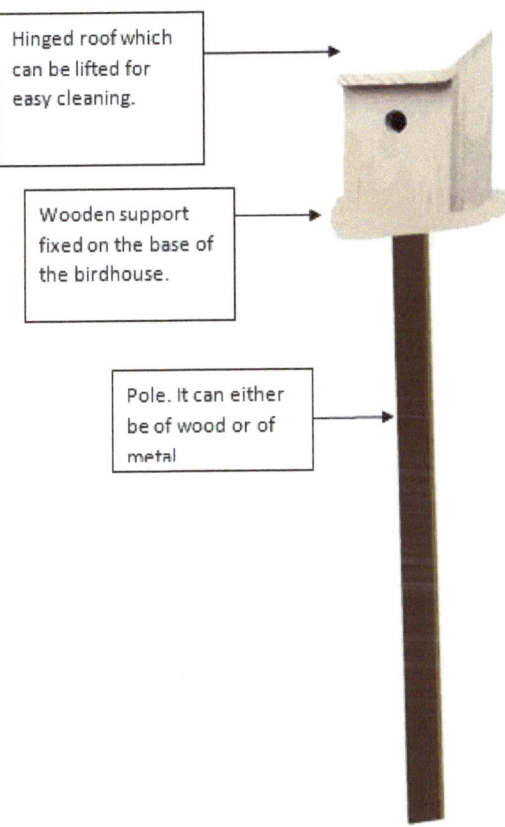

Hinged roof which can be lifted for easy cleaning.

Wooden support fixed on the base of the birdhouse.

Pole. It can either be of wood or of metal

You have a birdhouse, which can be placed either on a wooden or metal support or nailed to a safe and secure tree trunk.

Why would I not advocate the use of chemicals – paint- in order to make a birdhouse more attractive? Remember that the bird is looking for a natural hidey hole, so if you paint your birdhouse, it will not come within smelling distance. In the same manner, do not use metal while building your birdhouse. You will notice that there is a wooden planks support between the pole and the birdhouse. That is to reinforce the strength of the base on which the birdhouse rests. Also, remember that if you are using a metal pole support, these supports can grow hot. In fact, wooden supports are better, especially if you are living in a hot and dry climate.

5. This bird house is best placed about 10 -12 feet above the ground. If you are placing the birdhouse in a shrub, or you have nailed it on a tree, face the entrance near another shrub or the nearest tree.

Maintenance of the Bird Box

Proper cleaning is necessary around February. Also repair these boxes before you mount them up on their perches again. Birds prefer nesting in really green and woody areas.

Enjoy watching your friends, nesting in their comfortable, sturdy and spacious bird house.

Taking Care Of Your Bird Pets

If you want to keep your feathered friends healthy and happy, remember that birds are social. So if you have a pair in a bird cage, they are going to keep each other company. On the other hand, if you just have one solitary bird, do remember to talk to it occasionally. That is, if you want to teach it how to talk, especially if it is a parrot or a hill mynah.

The idea of a spinster with caged bird and cat is clichéd, but birds are good companions for solitary people. Or anyone else for that matter, including invalids who are restricted to their rooms or are bedridden. Or anyone else who just wants to say something even if the audience is a bird (or a dog or a cat…).

I remember an instance as a child when I was not picking up so well after a bad attack of measles and fever. My grandfather immediately let our 6 pet lovebirds (budgerigars) into the closed room and told me to catch them and then cage them. The birds enjoyed the exercise in that small room. (They were used to be set loose in rooms and flying about. Then they sat on a curtain rail and demanded to be put back in their cage, when tired.) I enjoyed the exercise trying to catch them. This toned up my system wond'rously!

Please make sure that the pets you keep do not come under the Endangered Species Act.

I remember a neighbor who thought it very stylish to have a parrot as a pet. Those were the days when you did not have animal right activists protesting against caged birds in our city, and country. So she bought it, and caged it in an opulent cage. And then she forgot that parrots need company so the whole family left the poor thing locked up throughout the day where it squawked all alone to its heart's content. When the neighbors started to complain, she decided on something more unacceptable. She hung it outside so that the parrot could watch the world go by and other people would come and say hello to it.

I heard the bird squawking and went out to see what the matter was. There was absolutely no water in the cage. That foolish person had been told by someone that water should be changed only when the bird finishes the water already present in the container. I was so angry that I changed the water and got some more fresh stock of fruit, red chilies and sunflower nuts for it. She saw me and came squawking out of her house just like her parrot, and full of righteous indignation. How did I dare to interfere with her pet? How dare I touch it? How dare I give it food and water? After all, she had fed and watered it just 2 days ago. I was a nosy Parker, I was, and other statements of that ilk. Unfortunately, at that time, the SPCA was not active in our city. Otherwise it would have taken away that parrot. Also, she was watching me closely, so I could not indulge in some parrot – napping.

Luckily-I believe, for that parrot, – it developed a bad cough, because she had placed it in a draught. When I told her that her parrot was sick, I was told to MYOB in no uncertain terms and the parrot was just playing up to gain some attention. The poor little bird died in about five days, as I had predicted, but as I was away on a vacation, she could not blame me for possibly having done away with it as a mercy release. You never know!

So please do not be like that lady. It is no use buying a pet JUST because the Joneses are doing that, if you do not know how to take care of these birds.

If you have a bird, do not place it in the sun or in a draught. Imagine you in captivity with the sun beating down on your head. Also, imagine you shivering away in a draught, just because your master thought you needed some fresh air. Birds are as prone to cough and colds as we are. If you really want to give your bird some sunshine, hang him in the open air, but in the shade. It should also be out of the reach of predators. Make sure the cage door is secure.

Sawdust is the best possible absorbent material to place at the bottom of the cage. People also place sand there, but remember that birds occasionally eat that sand. So if the sand is filthy and is not changed very often, you are going to have a sick bird on your hands. I would suggest that you put the sand in a small bowl in his cage. So he can eat it along with his food in order to have enough of roughage in his crop to digest his meal. Do not place that bowl under the perch. The sand on the floor should be just enough to allow it to indulge in an occasional sand bath to get rid of all the mites, ticks and bird parasites.

Please change the water and add food to its bowl without fail, at least once or twice every day.

Twice during hot weather. If the water bowl is big enough, you may find your buddy having a bath in the bowl. So to make sure that it does not use its drinking water as a bathtub, make sure the size of the bowl is just large enough to hold water, but not large enough to hold the bird.

If your bird enjoys green vegetables and fruit, take away the food after it has eaten its fill. That prevents it from suffering from possible food poisoning due to have eaten stale food.

Feeding Your Feathered Friends

What do birds love to eat?

If you intend to make sure that your bird friends have plenty of free things to eat, especially during the winter, you need to make up a mixture of the things they love best. Unfortunately we do not have a plentiful supply of insects available to us in the winter – or, in the summer for that matter – to be chopped up – a man's work – and placed on the bird feeder.

Make sure that the bird feeder is large and sturdy enough to hold food as well as water. It should be able to bear the weight of a number of little squabbling birds just pouncing on that self-same morsel targeted by their best friends. If you do not happen to be living in a place covered by snow, I would suggest using the windowsill of a room as your bird feeder. Not only is this a sturdy base, but your birds begin to recognize this as a place where they are going to get plenty of things to eat and drink at regular intervals of time. You may even train them to come to you at the sound of a whistle. Last winter I used to call my bird friends with the help of a gray squirrel whistle. No gray squirrels turned up, but plenty of bird regulars spent a good winter eating birdseed, some pieces of dried coconut, even dried chilies and bread pieces, and I found that other squirrels really enjoyed rice and even beans. If you can eat anything cooked or raw, birds can too.

Do you have some extra suet in your larder? It is high-protein bird food, which is loved by your regulars as well as migratory birds. Birdseed is already an incentive for your birds to appear on your bird table regularly, but add a bit of suet and watching them invite their friends, relatives, and everyone around them to enjoy this energy giving diet.

Some of the bird species which love suet include blue jays, mockingbirds, chickadees, wrens, and other small and medium-sized bird species.

You can normally get premixed birdseed and birdfeed based on suet in the shops in your city, but it is very easy to make a suet recipe for your birds right there at home. I normally save bacon dripping and blend it myself to a smooth consistency or ask my butcher to grind the suet so that it is easy to make into balls or other shapes. I then heat it a bit to liquid level before I add in seeds, chopped nuts, pieces of fruit, and even any green leftovers from the kitchen. Once I added honey and some wheat flour and the birds loved it.

Once that suet mixture is properly mixed, refrigerate it. It will keep a long time, especially in the winters. Whenever you have to feed your birds, remove a chunk of this mixture, crumble or chop it into peck sized pieces and watch them go!

Why do birds love food with suet in it? That is because this is the best energy giving substance needed for migratory species. That is why I start feeding my bird pets suet meals from late fall itself. That is because I know that they will be going north or going south in the winter and they need energy boosters like suet to keep them happy and healthy. And also so that they come back to me safe and sound in spring next year.

Are you afraid of predators attacking birds when they are feeding? Well, you need to be on the lookout for crows, jays and other larger birds bullying and attacking smaller birds during feeding times. I also make sure that there is another feeder for pigeons on which I keep just birdseed. But I noticed wrens feeding from the pigeon feeder without bothering about the bigger birds. That is where agility and natural ability comes into play!

Starting A Bird watching Club

If you are interested in the secret life of birds, all you need to have is a little bit of patience, a little bit of interest in your bird friends and you can start bird watching, right in your garden itself. If you are lucky enough to have plenty of greenery near your home, you can go out for long walks armed with a pair of binoculars and a picnic basket [this last one is optional.] Make sure that you are wearing sturdy walking boots.

You can start a bird watching club in your city or in your locality, by asking other like-minded enthusiasts to join in your bird watching activities. You may want easy access to a good recorder, especially when you hear some bird song, which has never been heard in the vicinity before. Then you and your friends can compare notes.

Some bird species are very shy, while other bird species like to stay near human beings. These birds' species which prefer the company of human beings include sparrows, swallows and pigeons. These bird species do not mind sharing human inhabitation. Other birds are totally wild like the Eagle and can only be "domesticated" when they are hand reared as babies by experienced ornithologists and zoologists.

Rearing a wild baby bird by hand is not advisable if you do not have the experience and do not know much about that bird species habits. Yes, the temptation is there. You see this poor little featherless fledgling just fallen out from its nest and no parents around. You bring it home, wrap it up in cotton wool, and feed it protein and honey drops with the help of an eyedropper. But in most of the cases, the bird dies, because it is too weak to survive and also because it is too young and you are not its natural parent. So you end up with heartbreak.

This advice does sound cruel, but you need to follow it because even if a chick has been hand reared successfully, it will not survive in the wild. It can only survive in a zoo or in captivity. If it is left in the wild, it cannot fend for itself, because it was brought up in the company of humans and not of other birds of its own species. Also a chick which has been touched by a human hand is not going to be touched by its parents when it is placed back in the nest.

There are plenty of bird watching forums on the Internet. You may want to look for a bird watcher club right in your city.

Bird photography is a good and enjoyable pastime, if you have access to a good camera, accompanied by a powerful zoom lens.

Where can you find birds in the wilderness?

Many keen bird watchers say that they prefer to stay overnight in the woods, so that they can wake up at dawn and watch birds, which are normally not found in the cities. If you have the adventurous spirit to do that, please go right ahead. You may find yourself spending your weekends bird watching. But if you cannot bear the thought of staying in the woods at night, wake up early in the morning and go out for a walk in the wilderness. You may just be lucky enough to watch your bird leave its nest to catch the early worm.

I remember one of my friends being turned down for our amateur birds watching club even though she was a keen enthusiast and her knowledge of birds was considerable. That was because she had the habit of squeaking with excitement, and then moving whenever she saw a new bird species. It used to scare the nonexistent trousers off the bird which went winging away chirping in terror. And then she would give us a sheepish apologetic smile and say "Sowwy". (I did not tell you that she occasionally lisped too, especially when she was embarrassed and she was subjected to the EVIL Eye by anywhere between 6 to 12 keen and thoroughly annoyed birdwatchers.) Otherwise, she was quite a sensible and level-headed person in all other respects. It was just when she saw birds in the wilderness, she went squeak squeak to the tune of "ohloookloolklook there, there, on that branch" in what she hoped to be a whisper and then "Sowwy". This is an extreme case, but then even the most patient of bird watchers can lose their tempers when they are confronted with such – according to them immature and childish – behavior. So we turned down her application to join our bird watching club, because we were too law-abiding to resort to a gag when she accompanied us.

So enjoy your bird watchers club and note down the species you can recognize. We normally try to identify the birds with these notes –

- Size of the Bird – small, medium, large.

- Color of plumage – look at the head, neck, wings, body and back. If the bird flew away, was the underside of the wing of a different color?

- Where did you see it? – On the ground, in a shrub, on a tree?

- Date of viewing –

- Who saw it along with you? What are the details about the bird which he can add? Did you record its bird song? Do you take a photograph?

You can add any other data which you can think relevant. Who knows, you may come up with a totally unknown bird species. Best of luck.

Conclusion

Bird watching and getting to be friends with your feathered neighbors can be quite an enjoyable and relaxing pastime. In fact, many people who have retired find watching the birds in their garden to be quite a soothing experience. With the birdhouse building projects given in this book, you can build bird houses and bird feeders. Taking care of your bird pets will ensure happy companionship for you in this mutually satisfying Association.

So the next time you hear a bird song which you have not heard before, or you see a strange bird in your garden or in your neighborhood, just take some time off your busy, busy, busy, hectic lifestyle and schedule and just stop and listen. You may be on the threshold of the magical world of birds.

Common bird species universally found all over the world are crows, jays, wrens, hummingbirds, sparrows, Eagles, kites, Swallows, Swifts, Owls, and of course domesticated poultry like turkeys, ducks, geese, etc. Migratory birds may visit your country once a year, so if you are lucky enough to see those migrating birds it is going to be another memorable experience to add to your bird watching memories. These migrating birds include ducks, geese, cranes, Eagles, Gulls, Wrens, Buntings, Swallows, Swifts and Snipes' species depending on your proximity to water – Lakes, swamps – and warm weather in the winter.

All bird species do not migrate. Sedentary bird species which live in your area may move a small distance away for safety reasons or by looking for better feeding grounds. But they are going to stay within their territory as far as possible.

So now that you know what an enjoyable experience it is to begin this new relaxing activity of bird watching, is not it time you enjoy the company of your feathered friends while you can?

Author Bio

Dueep Jyot Singh is a Management and IT Professional who managed to gather Postgraduate qualifications in Management and English and Degrees in Science, French and Education while pursuing different enjoyable career options like being an hospital administrator, IT,SEO and HRD Database Manager/ trainer, movie scriptwriter, theatre artiste and public speaker, lecturer in French, Marketing and Advertising, ex-Editor of Hearts On Fire (now known as Solctice) Books Missouri USA, advice columnist and cartoonist, publisher and Aviation School trainer, ex- moderator on Medico.in, banker, student councilor ,travelogue writer … among other things! One fine morning, she decided that she had enough of killing herself by Degrees and went back to her first love -- writing. It's more enjoyable! She already has 24 published academic and 11 fiction- in- different- genre books under her belt.

When she is not designing websites or making Graphic design illustrations for clients who want Walt Disney, Norman Rockwell , JJ Grandville or Hed Kandy type illustrations, she is busy browsing in old bookshops for antique books,-she has a mouthwatering collection of priceless First editions and rare books…including R.L. Stevenson, O.Henry, Dornford Yates, Maurice Walsh, C.N.Williamson, and the crown of her collection- Dickens "The Old Curiosity Shop," and so on… Just call her "Renaissance Woman" - collecting herbal remedies, making one of a kind creations in Irish Crochet and Aran knitting, acting like Universal Helping Hand/Agony Aunt, or escaping to her dear mountains for a bit of exploring, collecting herbs and plants , trekking, and rappelling.

Illustrations and cartoons made by DJS.

Photos licensed by 123RF.com

Check out some of the other JD-Biz Publishing books
Health Learning Series

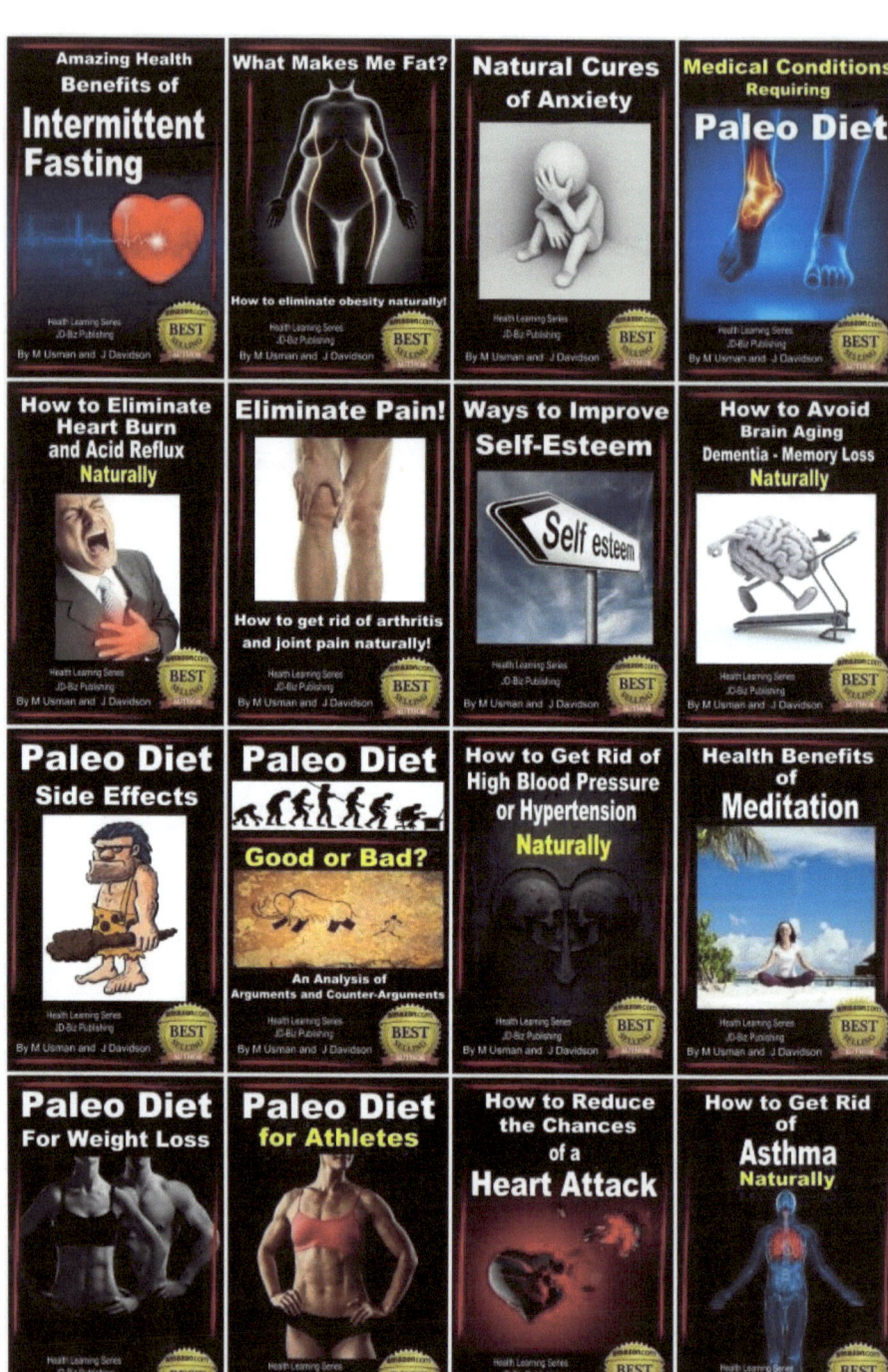

Amazing Animal Book Series

Learn To Draw Series

How to Build and Plan Books

Entrepreneur Book Series

Our books are available at

1. Amazon.com
2. Barnes and Noble
3. Itunes
4. Kobo
5. Smashwords
6. Google Play Books

Download Free Books!

http://MendonCottageBooks.com

Publisher

JD-Biz Corp

P O Box 374

Mendon, Utah 84325

http://www.jd-biz.com/

Mendon Cottage Books
P O Box 374, Mendon Utah 84325